The Adventures of Beckham Grey

All Stuffed

Copyright © 2023 Elizabeth Alfheim
with Julia Grant
Illustrated by Chad Thompson
All rights reserved.

ISBN: 979-8-9885419-2-9

Quail Acres Publishing
Imagination is Priceless!

www.elizabethalfheim.com

Printed and bound in the United States of America

What's Wrong with this Picture?

Can you find the 8 things that are wrong in this picture?
Look carefully. Circle all 8 if you can.

A-Mazing Dance Moves!

"Moo," Beckham encouraged, "come take my hand."
"We will dance, and it will be grand."

Help Moo find her way to Beckham Grey.

What's Next?

Look at the pictures in each row. Write the number of the picture from the list below that continues the pattern in the last box.

1, 2, 3 Practice

Practice writing your numbers by tracing the ones below. Then try a couple on your own.

1   1   1

2   2   2

3   3   3

4   4   4

5   5   5

6   6   6

7   7   7

Good job!
Circle your best number in each row.

8   8   8

9   9   9

10   10   10

A to Z Practice

Practice writing your letters by tracing the ones below. Can you sing the alphabet too?

Aa Bb Cc Dd Ee Ff

Gg Hh Ii Jj Kk Ll

Mm Nn Oo Pp Qq

Rr Ss Tt Uu Vv Ww

Xx Yy Zz

Good job!
Now try it again.

Aa Bb Cc Dd Ee Ff

Gg Hh Ii Jj Kk Ll

Mm Nn Oo Pp Qq

Rr Ss Tt Uu Vv

Ww Xx Yy Zz

Alpha Bear

Fill in the missing letters of the alphabet.

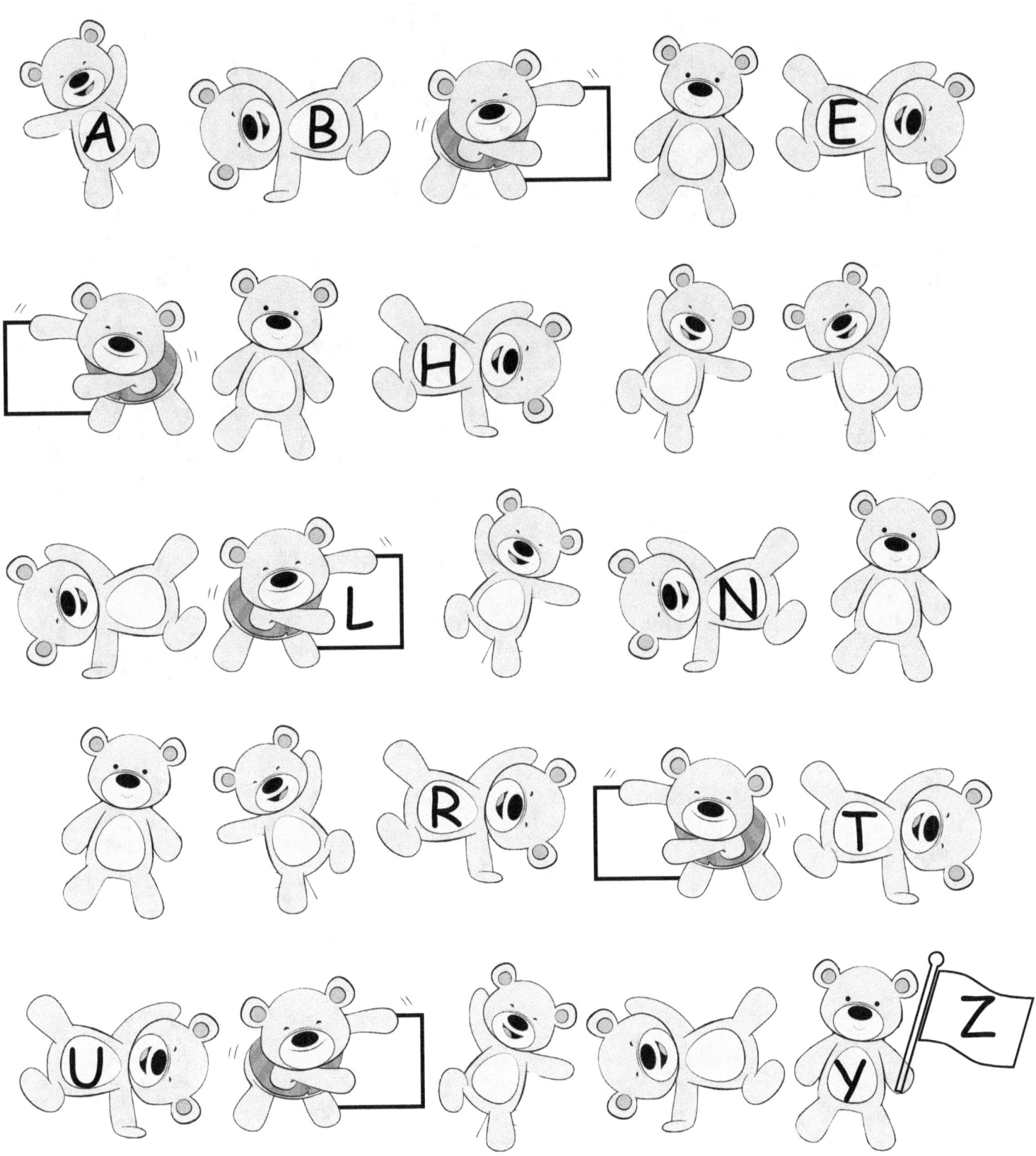

Alphabet Pairs

Draw a line to the matching letters to give Goat back his hat.

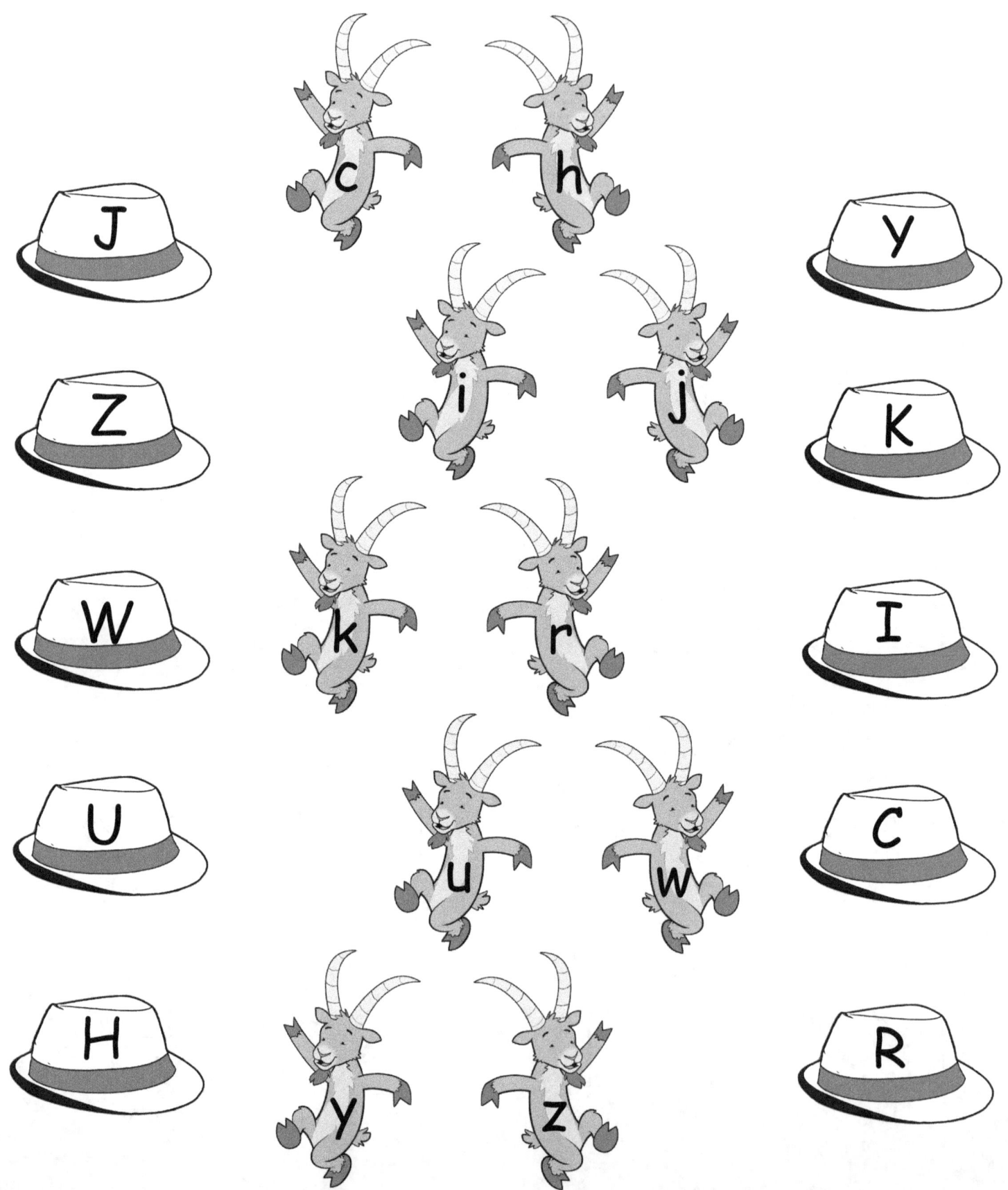

Beckham's Dance Challenge

How many animals are ready for a dance challenge? Put a tally mark in the box marked YES for each animal that is wearing dance attire. Put a tally mark in the box marked NO for each animal that is not ready. Cross out the animal once it has been counted. The first one is done for you. Then count all of the tally marks for each answer and write that number in the correct box.

YES	NO	YES total	NO total
	I		

BEFORE - Between - AFTER

Write the number that comes before, between, and after each number below.

BEFORE

___ 15

___ 2

___ 8

___ 19

___ 6

___ 5

___ 14

Between

1 ___ 3

9 ___ 11

5 ___ 7

12 ___ 14

15 ___ 17

10 ___ 12

3 ___ 5

AFTER

6 ___

19 ___

8 ___

16 ___

3 ___

9 ___

4 ___

Monkeying Around with Colorful Shapes

Look at each divided shape. Using the color code key, circle the shape with the correct color.

Color Code

green - 1 of 3 are shaded   **blue** - 1 of 4 are shaded

red - 2 of 3 are shaded   **orange** - 2 of 4 are shaded

Consonant Blends

ck   sh   tr   sk   ch

Write in the correct consonant blends in the spaces below. Use the letter combinations above. Then draw a line from each word to the correct picture.

_____oes

_____unk

_____irt

ba_____et

_____air

ro_____et

Count How Many

Count how many goats or hats are in each box.
Circle the correct number.

2 3

5 7

8 9

6 7

8 10

3 4

4 6

1 2

2 3

Counting by...

Write the number that you say when you count by 2's.

2 ____ ____ ____ ____ ____ ____

Write the number that you say when you count by 3's.

9 ____ ____ ____ ____ ____

Write the number that you say when you count by 5's.

20 ____ ____ ____ ____ ____

Write the number that you say when you count by 10's.

20 ____ ____ ____ ____ ____

Write the number that you say when you count by 100's.

200 ____ ____ ____ ____ ____

Circle the beginning sound for each object.

B D P V

B P D S

K D V H

L B C X

A K V R

Z S T F

Which is Bigger?

Circle the biggest animal in each row.

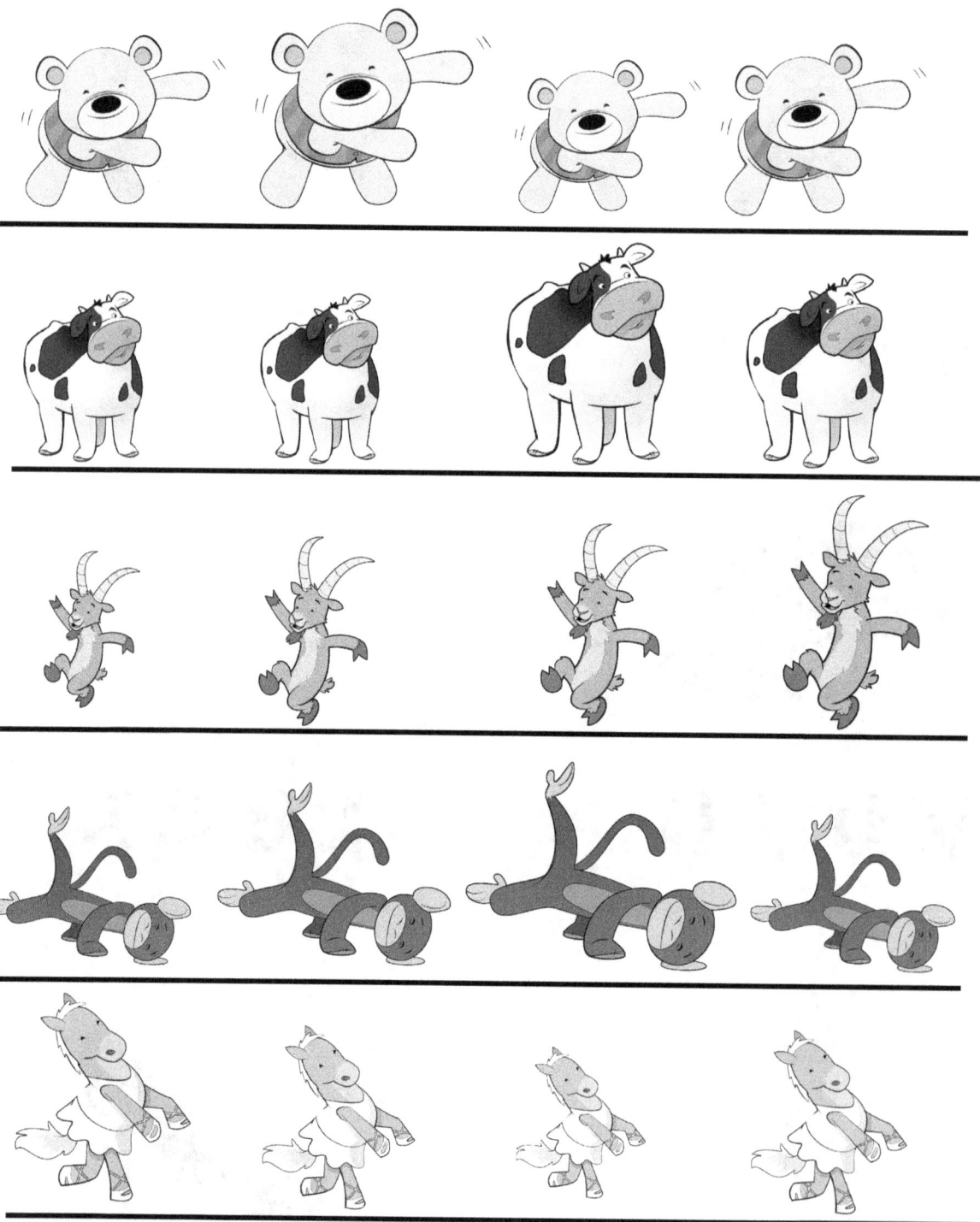

Adding 10

Connect Giraffe's string to the correct yoyo by adding ten.

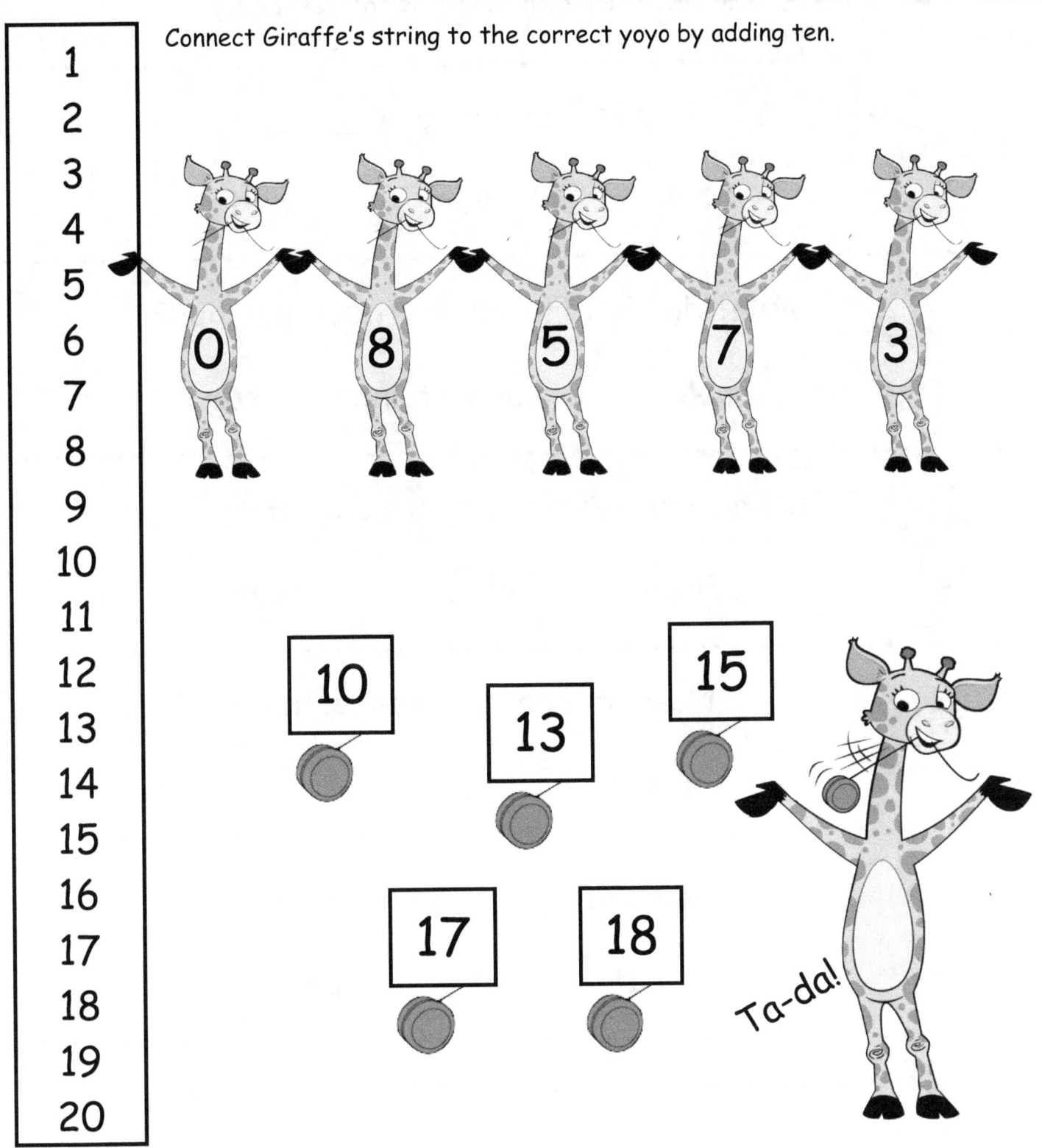

All Stuffed Full of Questions

Have you read the book *The Adventures of Beckham Grey: All Stuffed*?
Read each sentence and circle the best answer.

Bubba Bear sat on a _____.

book   chair   shelf

What did Giraffe put between her lips?

book   yoyo string   rug

Beckham and Bubba wrestled on the _____.

floor   chair   bed

Nosy strapped these on her feet.

gloves   shoes   clothes

Baa had a _____ on his head.

cat   hat   shoe

Moo didn't want to dance because she was _____.

clumsy   shy   busy

1 to 10 Practice

Practice writing your numbers and words by tracing the ones below. Count the BEARS in each line.

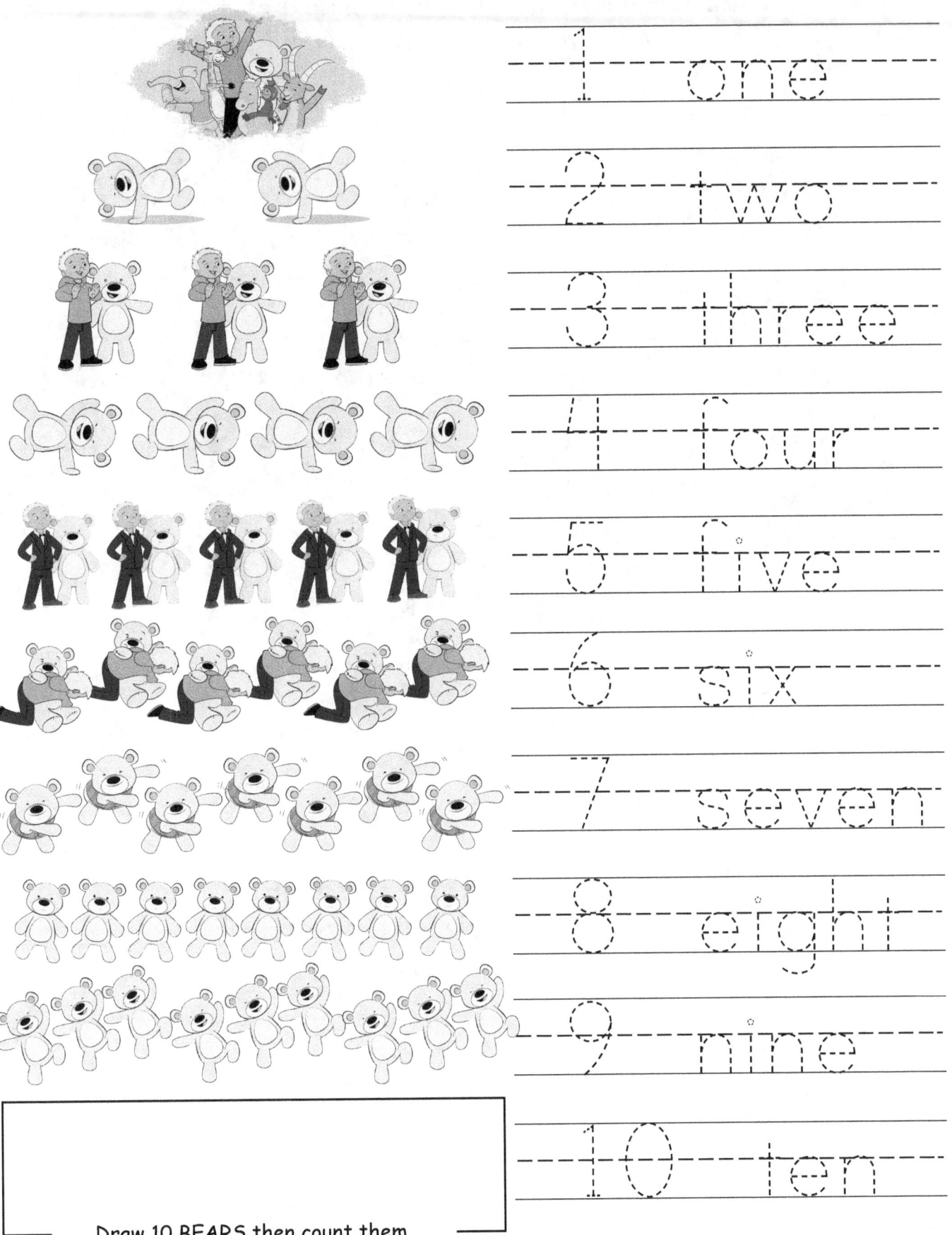

1 one

2 two

3 three

4 four

5 five

6 six

7 seven

8 eight

9 nine

10 ten

Draw 10 BEARS then count them.

Color 5 Dresses for Pony

Then count how many ponies have white dresses.
Write your answer in the box.

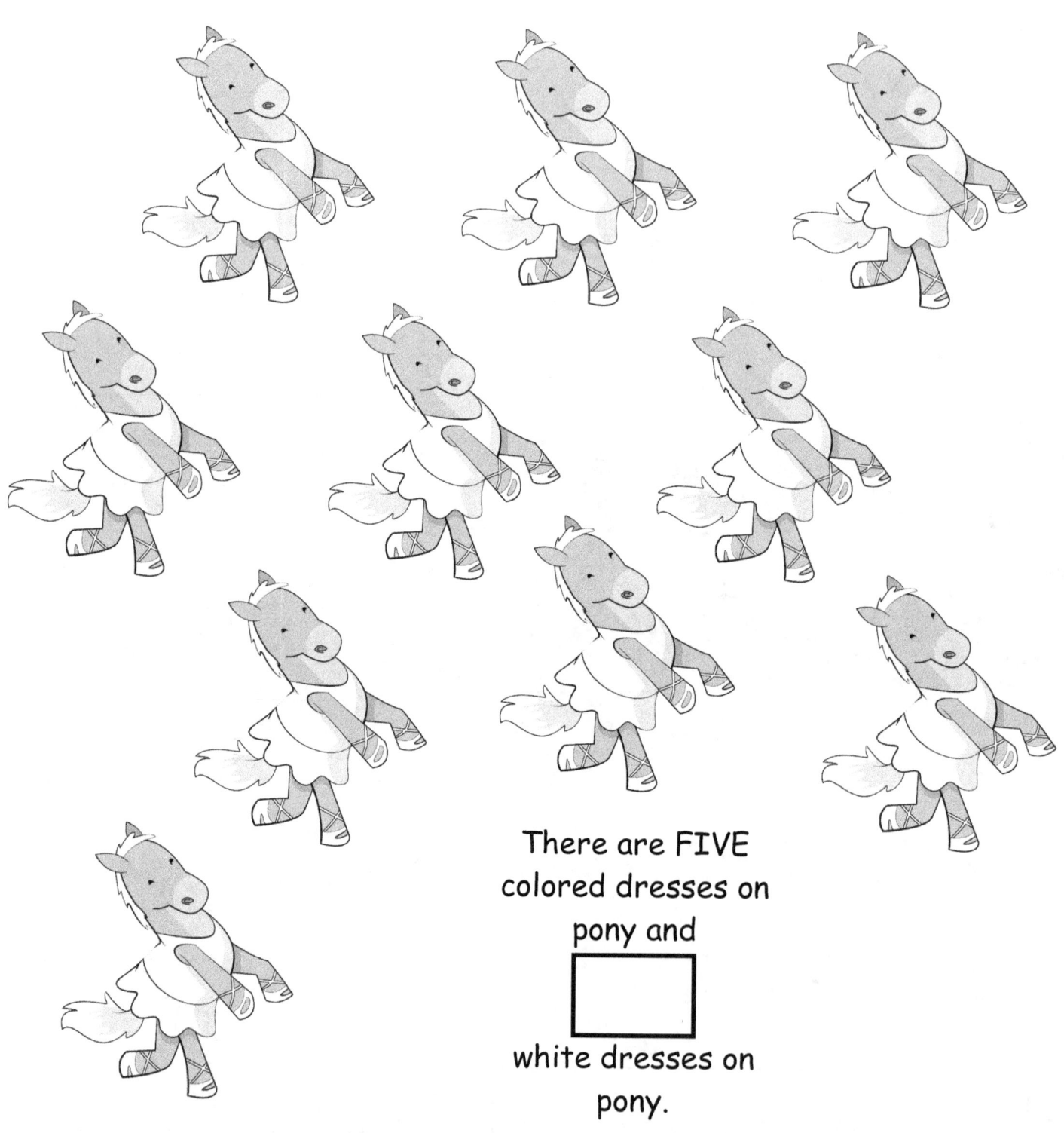

There are FIVE
colored dresses on
pony and

white dresses on
pony.

Go Go Giraffe

Color all of the giraffes with the number 17.

How many giraffes
with the number 17
did you find?
_____
- - - - - - - - -
_____

Groups of Seven

Draw a line from the number 7 to each group of 7.

Hidden Treasures

Can you find all of the 12 items listed?
Look carefully. Circle each one that you find.

key	star	desk lamp	letter B
hanger	hat	moustache	mitten
duck	baseball	arrow	sunglasses

How Many Do You Count?

How many items do you count in each row? Write the number in the box.

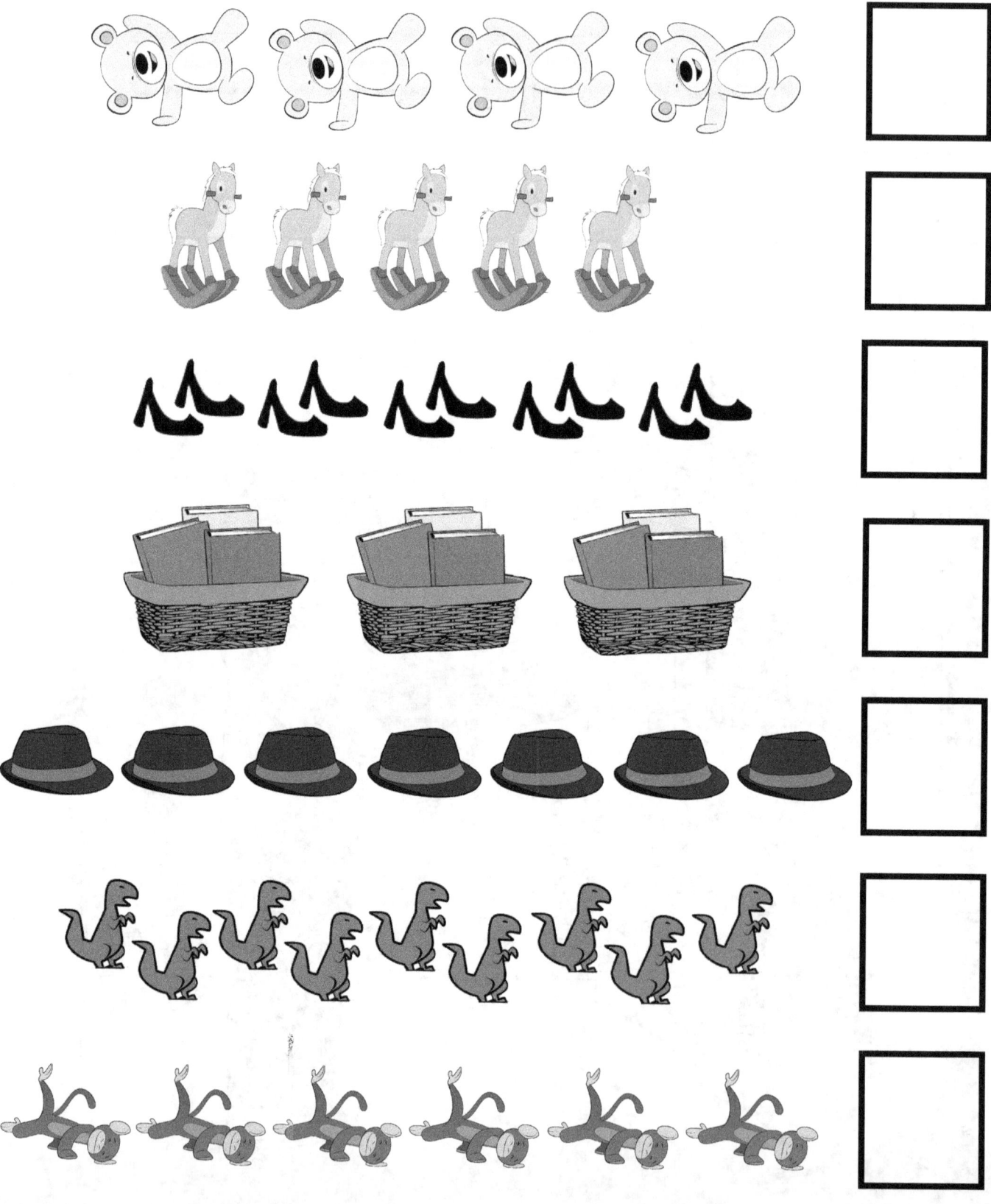

Main Idea

Look at each picture. Read each sentence.
Circle the sentence that best describes what is happening in the picture.

Beckham lost his teddy bear.	
Beckham is scared.	
Beckham is pondering.	

Beckham loves his giraffe.	
Beckham is hugging his elephant tightly.	
Beckham wants to play.	

Beckham is wrestling with his big bear.	
Beckham fell asleep on his bear.	
Beckham likes to eat waffles.	

Giraffe and Elephant tripped and fell on the ground.	
They are pretending to sleep.	
They are dancing.	

Help Goat Find His Hat

Measure It!

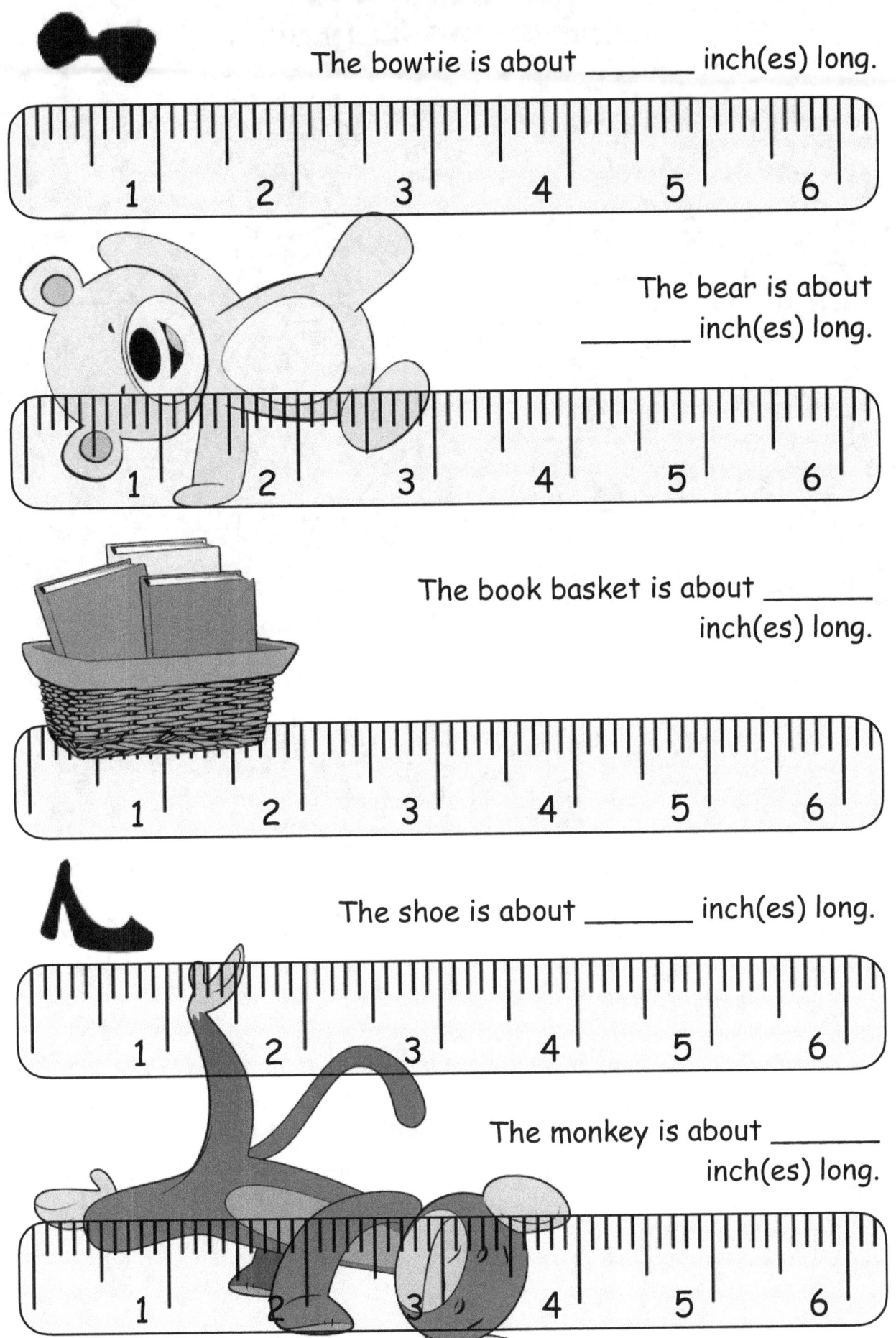

The bowtie is about _____ inch(es) long.

The bear is about _____ inch(es) long.

The book basket is about _____ inch(es) long.

The shoe is about _____ inch(es) long.

The monkey is about _____ inch(es) long.

Counting by 5's, fill in the MISSING numbers on the bear.

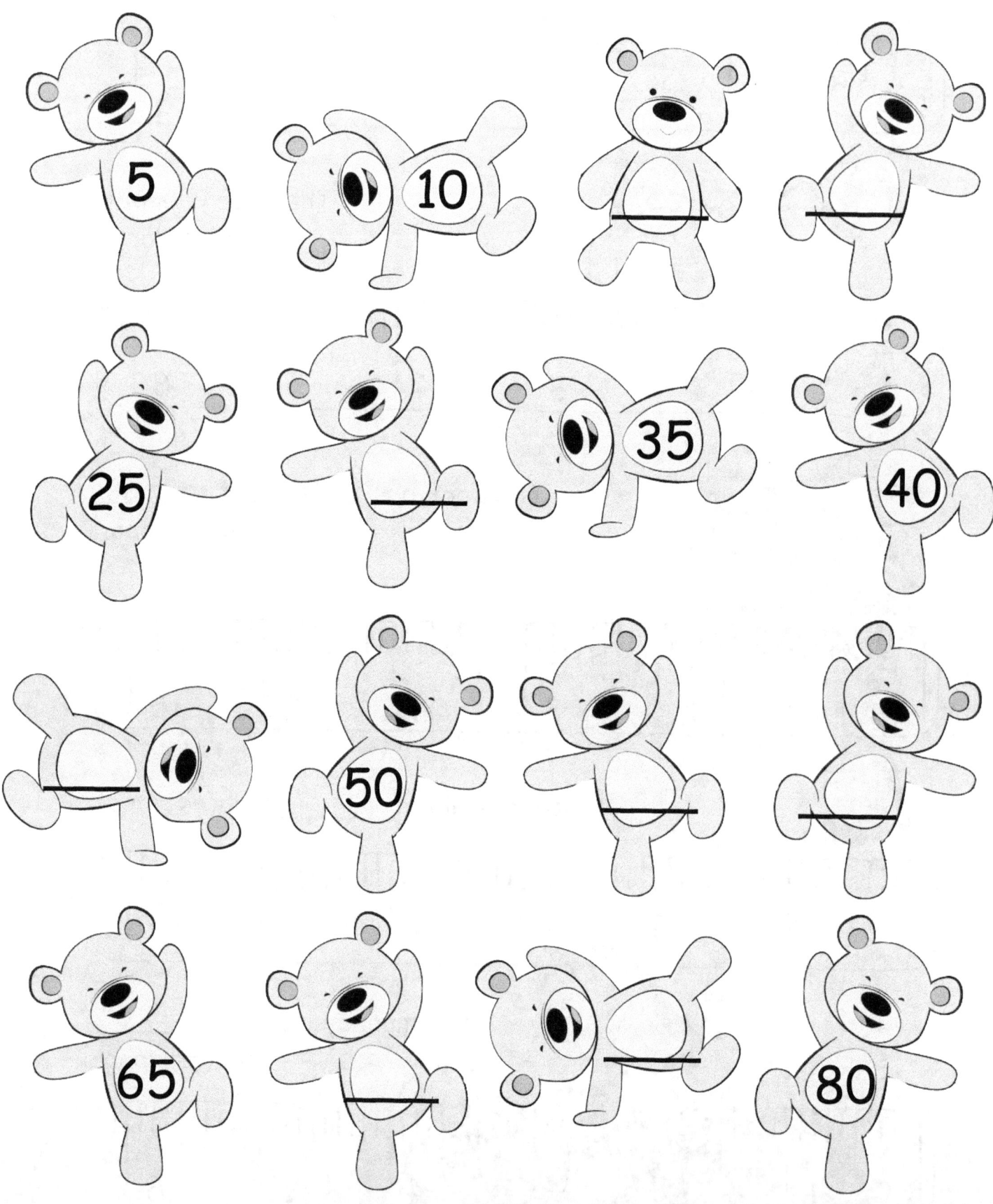

Identifying Verbs

A verb is an action word. It tells what a person, place, thing, or idea does.

The boy and the bear (wrestled) about.

Part 1

Directions: Circle the verb in each sentence.

1. Then, all the animals jumped for joy.

2. Beckham's face beamed brightly.

3. Holly the horse did a ballet act.

4. Giraffe performs the twist.

5. Sometimes it takes help from a friend.

Part 2

Directions: Write a sentence below. Circle the verb in your sentence.

_____

_____

_____

_____

Look, Practice, Spell

Look at the picture. **Practice** the beginning letter. **Spell** the word for each picture.

Bb   books

Dd   dinosaur

Ss   shoe

Gg   goat

Bb   bowtie

Gg   giraffe

Ee   elephant

Hh   hat

Mm   monkey

Rr   rocket

Gone Missing!

Directions: Oh no! WORDS have gone missing. Using the word bank, find the missing word to complete each sentence. Write it on the blank line.

> plucked   acquired   confidence
> gusty   budge   muster

Giraffe was _____ from the zoo.

The wind was _____ on this early spring day.

So, he just sat with the others; he didn't
_____ .

It all began when Bubba was _____ from his chair.

She couldn't
_____
the courage; she was too shy.

Moo had no _____ to dance at all.

Months of the Year

Fill in the missing months of the year.

January
February
March
April
May
June
July
August
September
October
November
December

January

March

April

June

September

November

Dancing Bears

Count the bears that are dancing. Count how many bears that have stopped dancing. Subtract to tell how many are still dancing with their friends.

Dot to Dot by 5s

Connect the dots to complete the picture.

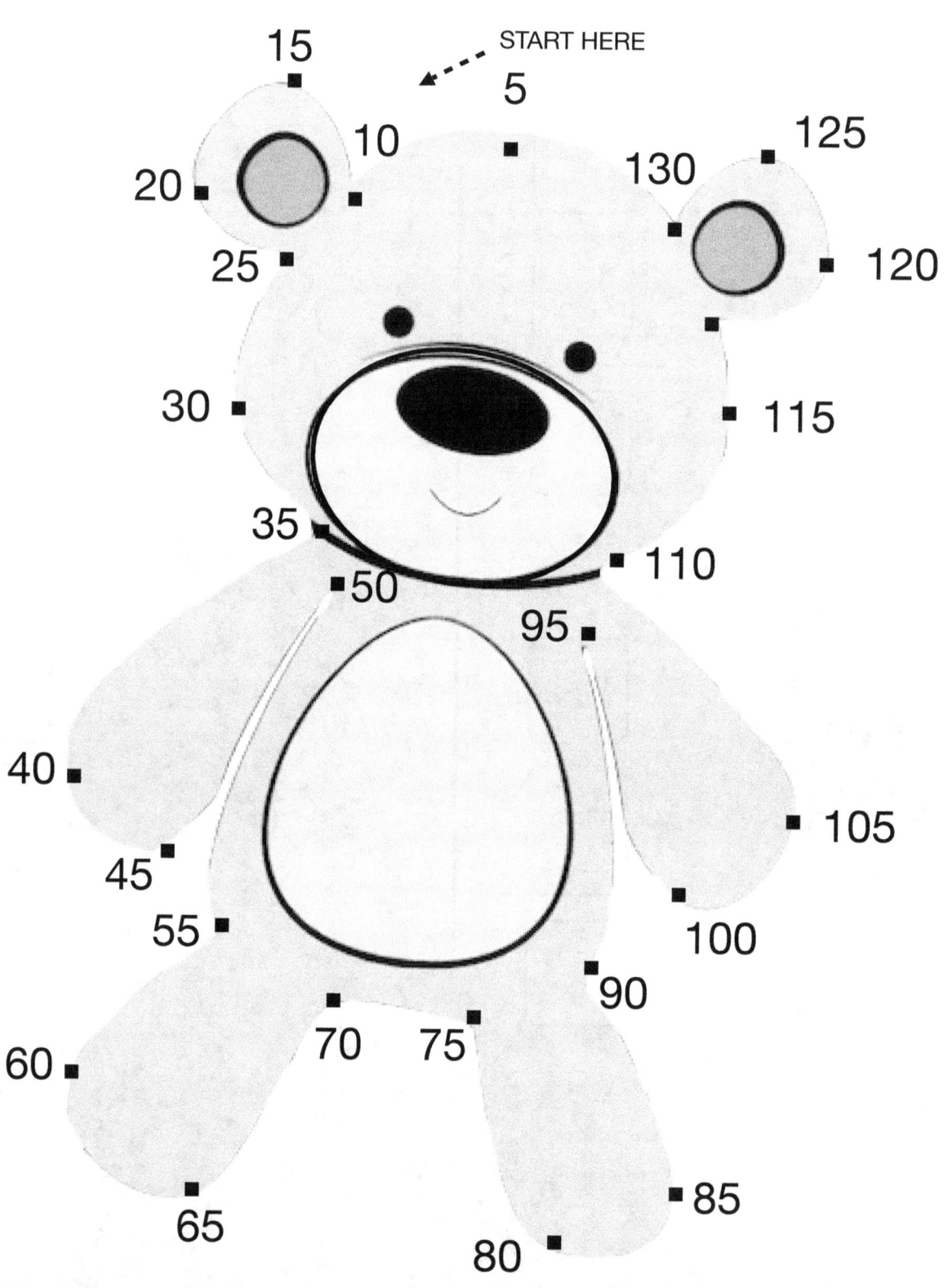

More or Less

Count how many in each group. Write the number on the line
below the group. Circle the group that has MORE.

 OR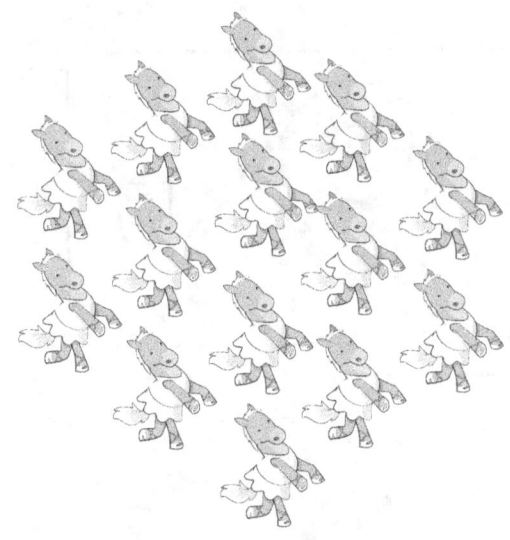

_____   _____

_____   _____

 OR

_____   _____

More or Less?

Compare the two numbers in each row. Trace the correct word "more" or "less" to complete the sentence correctly.

 is
more
less
than

 is
more
less
than

 is
more
less
than

 is
more
less
than

 is
more
less
than

Color every number five.
How many did you find?

Your Answer

NUMBER MAZE

Goat needs your help to find his hat so that he can wear it to the Dance Off.
Help him find it. Draw a path from Goat to his hat by counting from 1 to 20.

1	5	2	3
2	3	4	6
8	10	9	11	5	7
14	11	8	7	6	10
13	12	17	18	14	15
14	15	16	19
17	11	18	20

One Syllable Word Search

Find each word and circle it. Words can be across or down.

A	B	O	O	K	S
N	E	S	U	W	U
D	A	N	C	E	N
D	R	G	O	N	C
O	A	N	W	C	E
B	G	O	A	T	S

BEAR

SUN

GOAT

BOOKS

DANCE

COW

Out of Sight Words

Read it.

and

Say the word out loud.

Color it.

AND

Color the word.

Trace it.

and

Trace the word.

Clap it.

(1) (2) (3)

How many syllables are in the word?
Color in the correct number.

Write it.

Write the word.

Spell it.

Spell the word.

Find it.
Find the word and color it.

| and | ant | and |
| all | and | ade |

Say it, again!

and

a-n-d

Say the word, again.
Then spell it out loud.

Draw a line to connect the matching giraffes.

The Four Seasons

Oh no! The seasons are all scrambled.
Unscramble each word and write the correctly spelled
season next to it.

gnpirs _____

itrewn _____

mutnau _____

rmusme _____

A Picture is Worth A Thousand Words

For each word, read the description.
Then draw a picture that shows the word in action.

Gusty: Stormy; breezy.

The wind was <u>gusty</u> on this early spring day.

Threads: Clothing; garments.

They slipped on their shoes and their dancing <u>threads</u>.

Add 'Em Up Math

How many of each do you see? Add 'em up and write the total in the box.

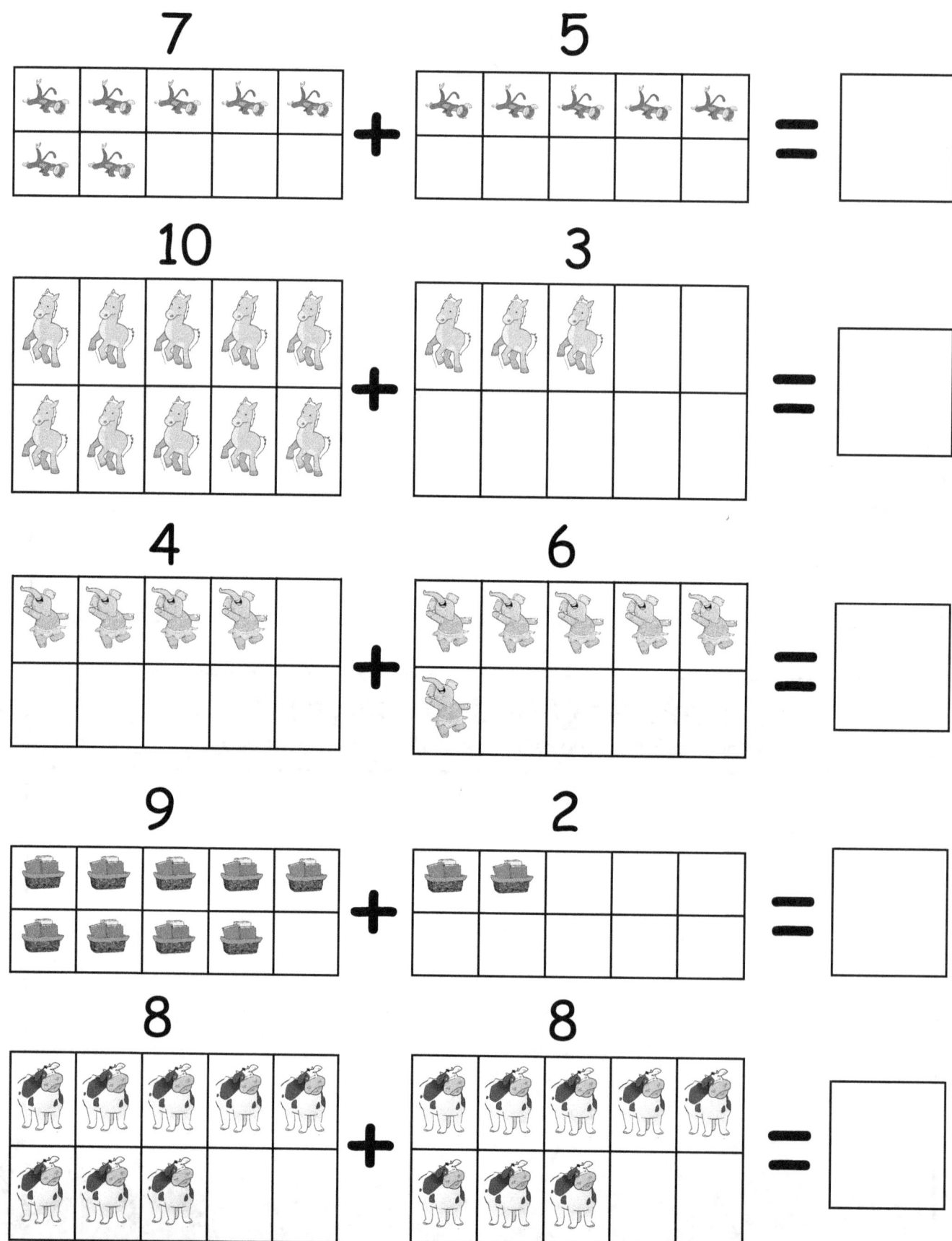

Skip Count by Ten

Each group has ten items in it. Count by tens and write the total in the box.

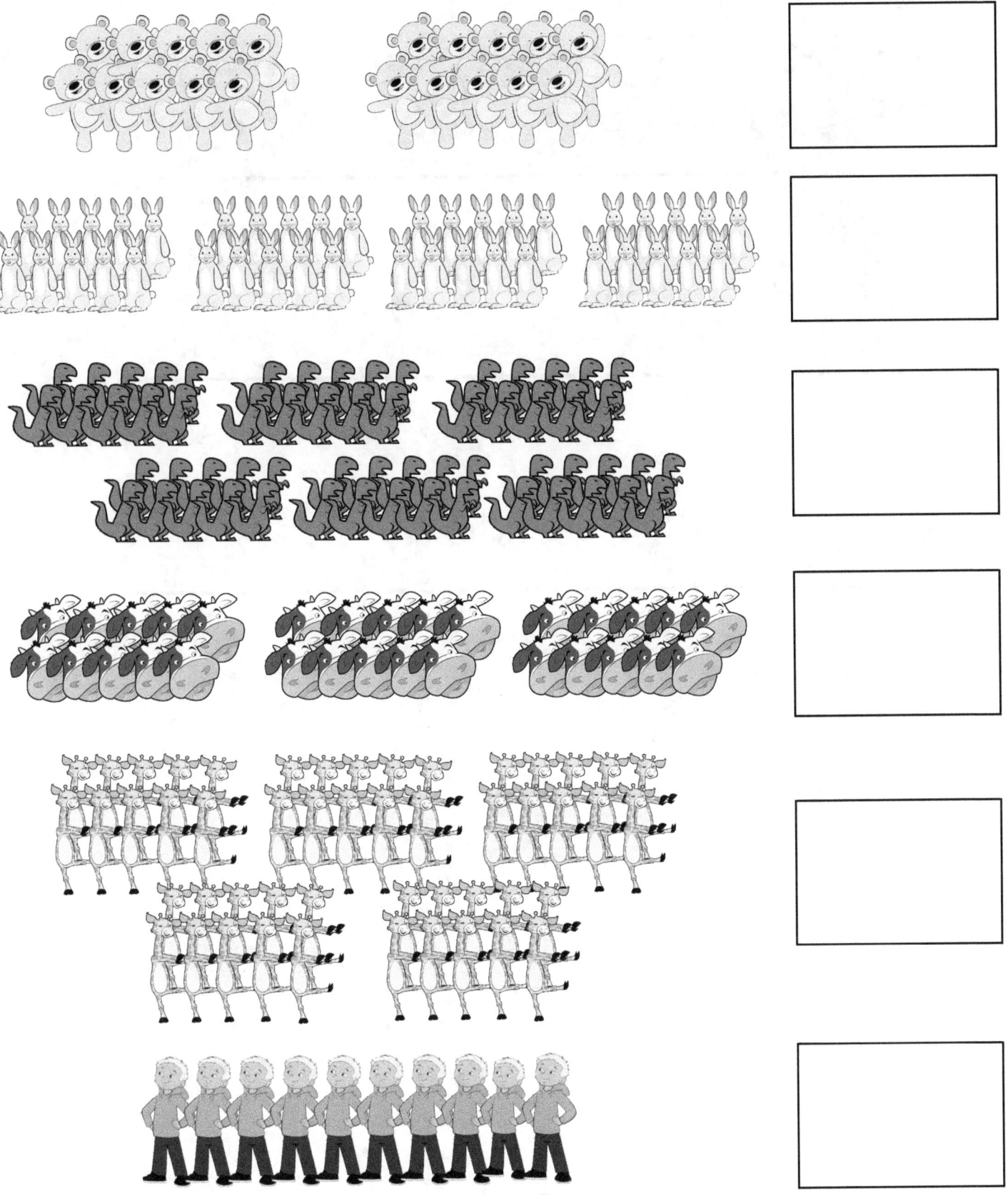

Which is Smaller?

Circle the smallest animal in each row.

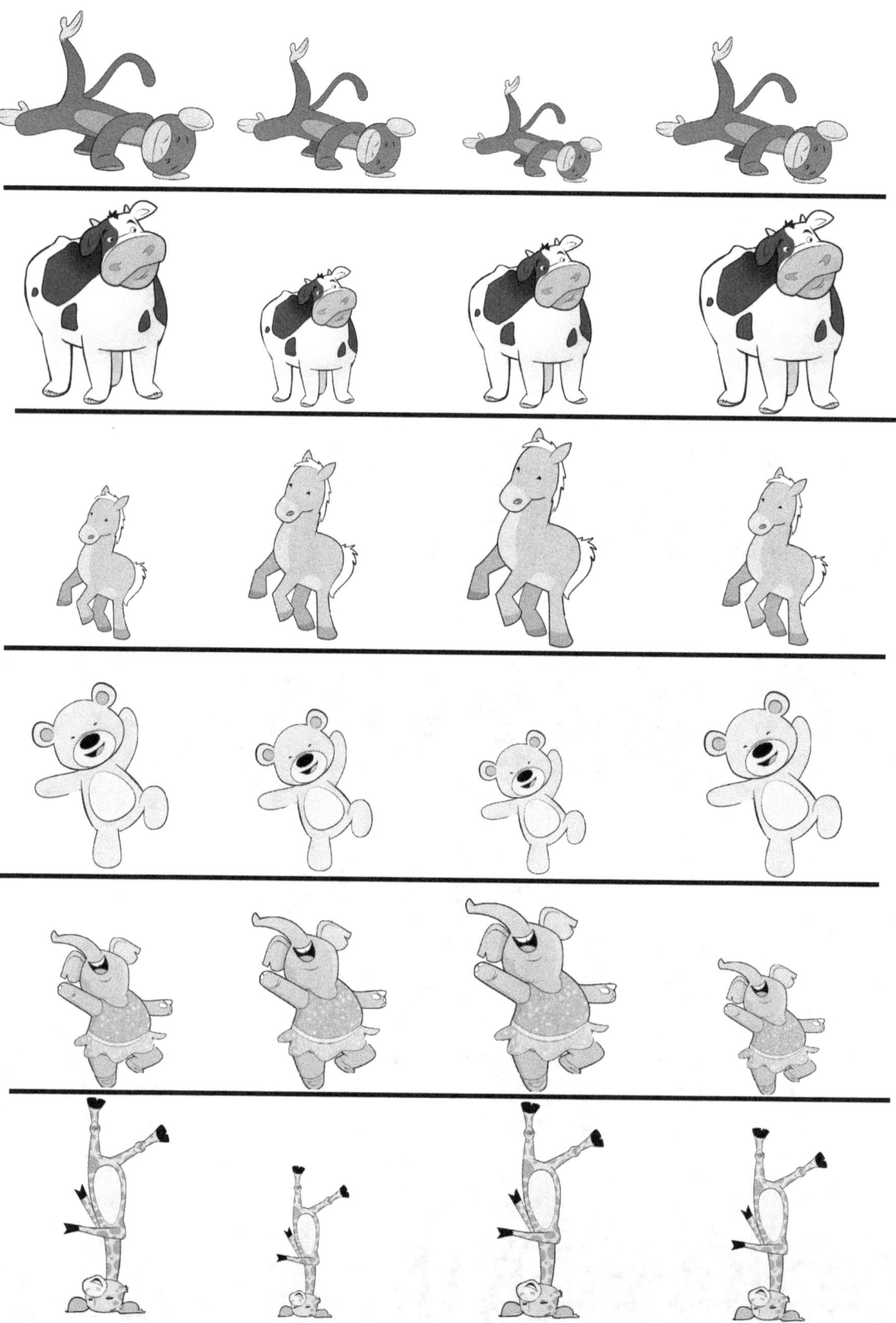

Something's Missing

Circle the picture in each row that has something missing.
Can you draw the missing parts?

Taking Shape

Practice tracing the shapes. Then color them.

Play Time Is Over

It's time to put away some toys. Circle the toys to match each number.

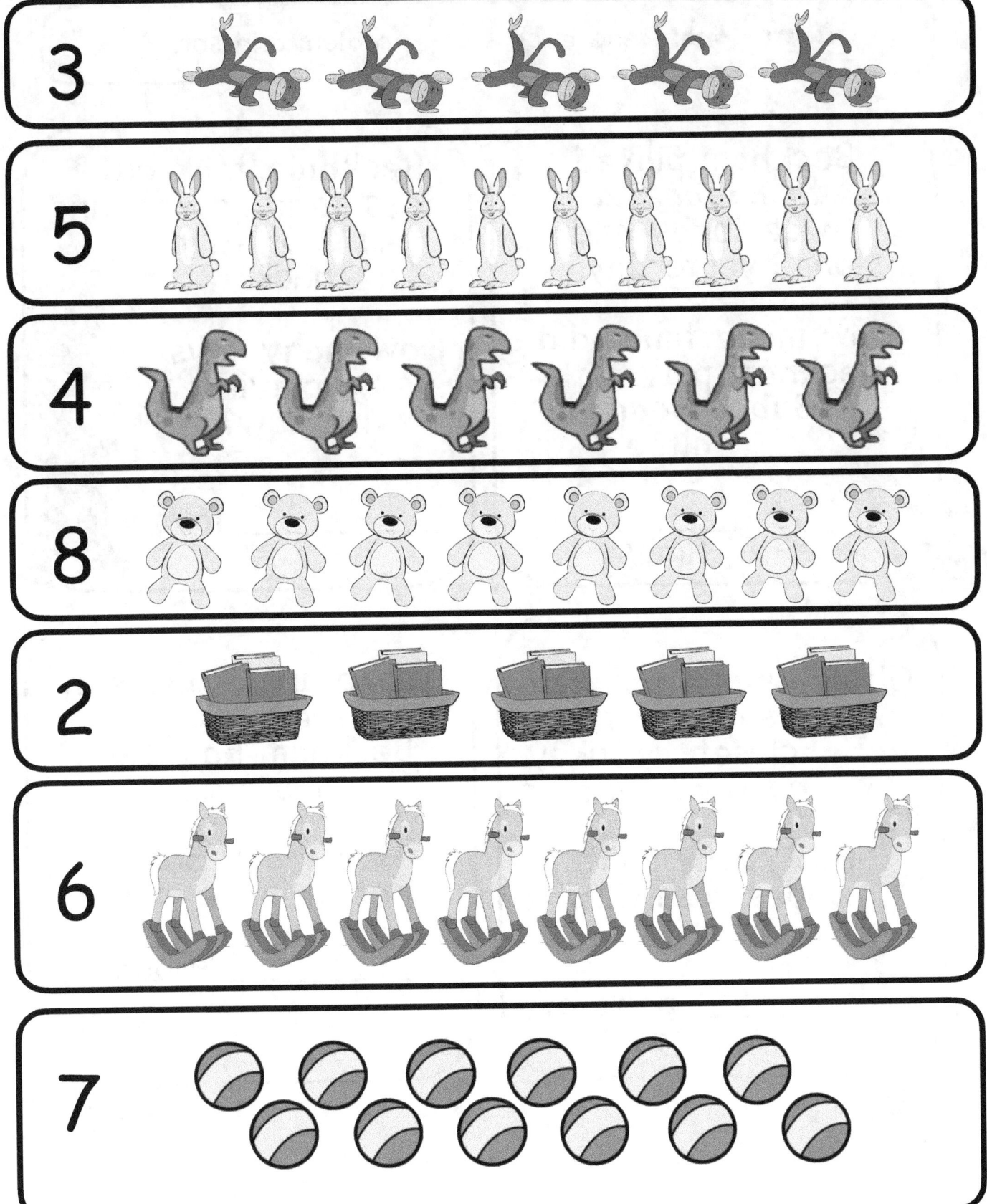

Problem Solving

Directions: Read each story problem and solve.

Beckham played with Bubba Bear twice today and once yesterday.

How many times did Beckham play with Bubba Bear in all?

_____ Times

Beckham took out 5 toys to play with and put 2 of them back.

How many toys is he playing with now?

_____ toys

Giraffe has 4 pairs of shoes in the closet. Monkey borrowed a pair.

How many pairs of shoes does Giraffe have left?

_____ pairs of shoes

There are 3 books in the basket. Beckham has 2 on his bed.

How many books does he have in all?

_____ books

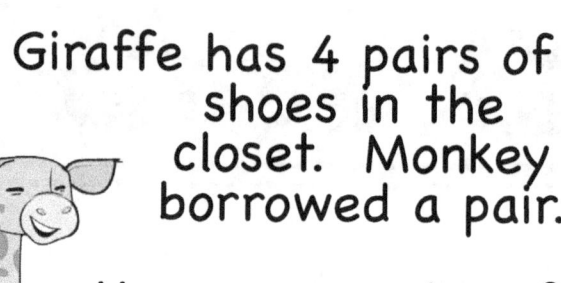

Rainbow Days of the Week

Practice writing the days of the week by tracing the ones below.
Then color the boxes.

red	1 Sunday
orange	2 Monday
yellow	3 Tuesday
green	4 Wednesday
blue	5 Thursday
dark blue	6 Friday
purple	7 Saturday

See and Play

Beckham loves to create stories and **play** with his stuffed animals.
Using the sight word **play**, complete each activity below.

Fill in the missing letters.

pla_

pl_y

_lay

Unscramble the letters and write the word.

lapy

_____

- - - - - - - - -

Find and circle the words. Can you find all five?

p	l	a	y	n	p
r	t	y	m	n	l
x	p	l	a	y	a
w	l	e	o	d	y
g	a	v	u	i	s
x	y	p	l	a	y

Color in the dots to connect the letters to spell **play**.

Read and copy.

I can play games.

_____

- - - - - - - - - - - - - - - - - - -

Counting by 5's, fill in the MISSING numbers on the bear.

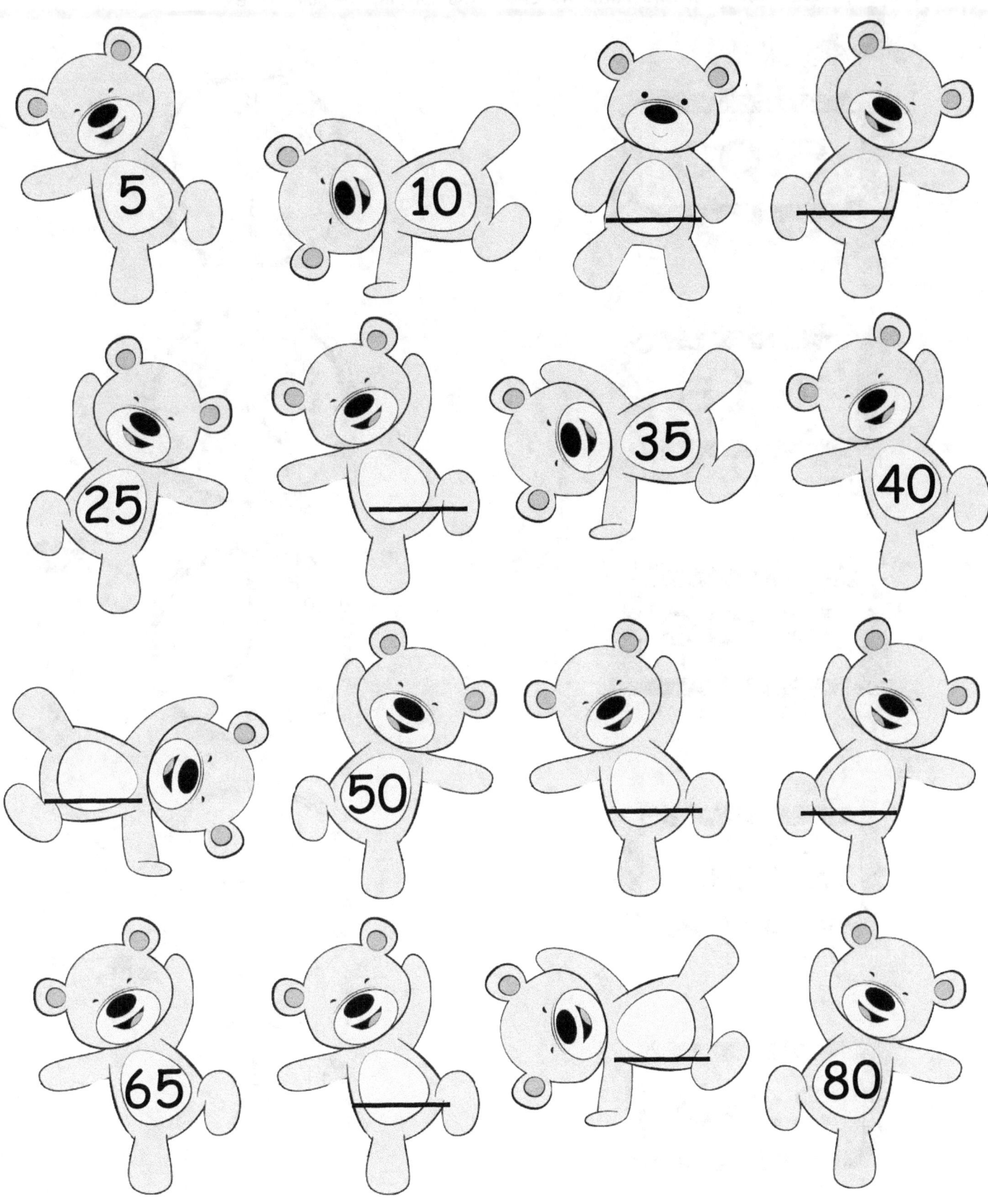

Telling Time

 **Draw** a line to match the clocks that display the same times.

5:00	
7:15	
12:00	
9:30	
2:30	

Shapes

Practice writing the names of shapes by tracing the ones below.
Then draw a line from the name of the shape to its matching shape.

- Circle
- Oval
- Rectangle
- Square
- Star
- Triangle

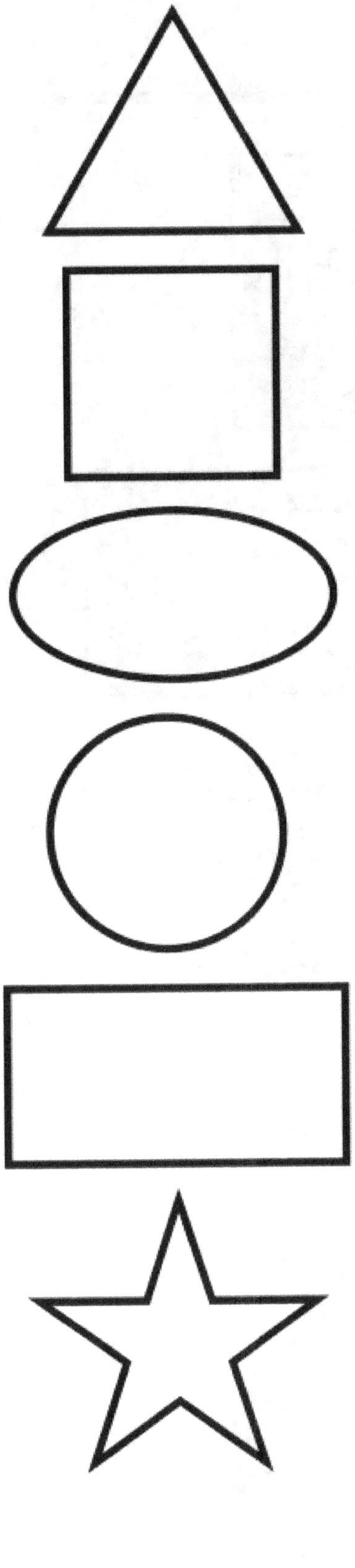

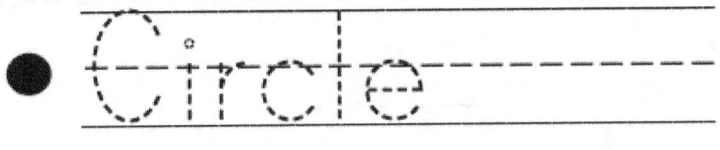

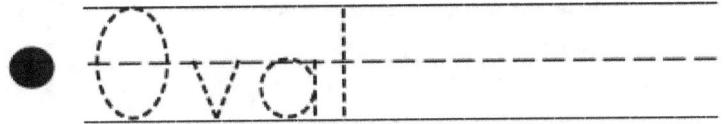

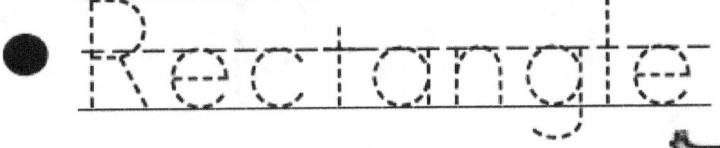

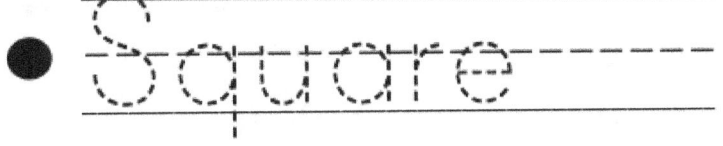

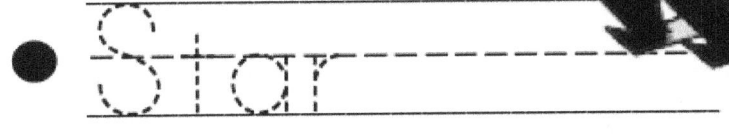

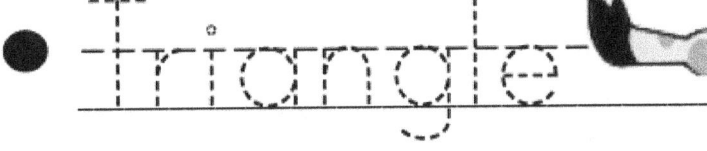

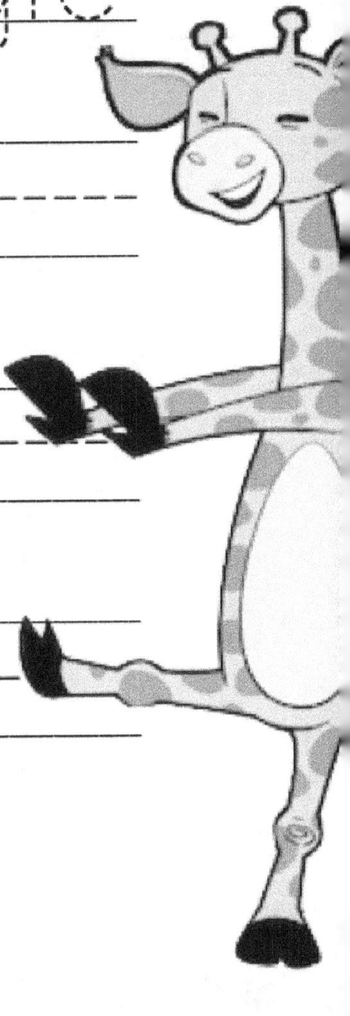

Short Vowel Sounds

a e i o u

Write the missing vowel for each word below.

b __ d

r __ g

p __ g

c __ t

d __ g

What's the Missing Letter?

There are missing letters in each sentence. Use the pictures as clues to fill in the missing letter.

1. __ows eat __rass in the meadow.

2. A __abbit chews on a __arrot.

3. The __onkey swings in the __ree.

4. The __loud is behind the __un.

5. The __oat dances to the __usic.

6. The __iraffe loves her dancing __hoes.

What's What?

Using the word bank at the bottom, identify each item or body part.
Write the word in the box.

knee	trunk	teeth	mouth
head	ear	belly	arm

UNSCRAMBLE

Use the picture to help you unscramble the letters.
Write the word in the space provided.

	esoh	-------------------
	kobos	-------------------
	tha	-------------------
	ypno	-------------------

What Weighs More?

Circle the object that is heavier.

Word Match

Help Beckham and Bubba Bear match the words to their definitions. Draw a
line from each word to its meaning.

Commence	Close.
Roar	Actively; with anticipation.
Neigh	New; current.
Eagerly	Unmistakable; specific.
Distinct	Moving from side to side; rocking.
Recent	Shout; holler.
Dear	Companion; friend.
Swaying	Begin; start.
Fellow	Fly; lift; rise.
Soar	Sound of a horse.

Word UP!

Do you know the word for each definition?
Need help? Refer to the Glossary in the book **The Adventures of Beckham Grey: All Stuffed**.

ACROSS
1. Cry; sob.
2. Fly; lift; rise.
3. Shriek; howl.
5. Great; glorious.
9. Shout; howl.
10. Clothing; garments.
11. Drift; idea.
12. Recommended; pushed.

DOWN
1. Brink; top.
2. Noticed; noted.
4. Sincere; honest.
6. Shout; holler.
7. Speak suddenly; blurt.
8. Exact; accurate.

Yes, We Can!

We can do a lot of things. Practice writing the word can.
Fill in the boxes. Then read what we can do.

can can

A bird ☐☐☐ fly.

A rabbit ☐☐☐ hop.

A cow ☐☐☐ moo.

A pony ☐☐☐ prance.

Beckham ☐☐☐ hug.

A cat ☐☐☐ run.

Can you write your own story?

Use any of the words below AND words of your own to write a story about the elephant. What is she doing? Where is she going? How would you describe her? Write your story on the lines below.

fun
shy
dances
elephant
happy
purple

teacher
learns
shoes
music
graceful
audience